by J. G. Minyard

Minneapolis, Minnesota

Credits
Cover, © Yaroslav Astakhov/Alamy Stock Photo; 4, © Gorodenkoff/Shutterstock; 4–5, © fpphotobank/ Getty Images; 5T, © Laurence Dutton/iStock; 5B, © Russell Hart /Alamy Stock Photo; 6, © GoodLifeStudio/ Getty Images; 6–7, © Antonio__Diaz/Getty Images; 8, © Witthaya Prasongsin/Getty Images; 9, © Westend61/Getty Images; 10, © EvgeniyShkolenko/Getty Images and © Bits And Splits/Shutterstock; 11, © gorodenkoff/Getty Images; 12, © Chaosamran__Studio/Shutterstock; 13, © Dragos Condrea/Getty Images; 14, © Aflo Co. Ltd. /Alamy Stock Photo; 15, © PeopleImages.com - Yuri A/Shutterstock; 16, © gorodenkoff/Getty Images; 17, © skynesher/Getty Images; 18, © AaronAmat/iStock; 18–19, © Wavebreak Media Premium /Alamy Stock Photo; 20, © Prostock-Studio/iStock and © gorodenkoff/iStock; 20–21, © NanoStockk/iStock; 22, © Maskot/Getty Images; 23, © Edwin Tan/Getty Images; 24, © Framestock/ Adobe Stock; 25, © Pixel-Shot/Shutterstock; 26, © whitebalance.oatt/Getty Images; 27, © adamkaz/Getty Images; 28TL, © janiecbros/iStock; 28TR, © PeopleImages/iStock; 28BL, © Pekic/Getty Images; 28BR, © ATHVisions/iStock; 29, © UPI/Alamy Stock Photo; 31, © spaxiax/iStock; 32, © Hajrudin Agic/iStock.

Bearport Publishing Company Product Development Team
Publisher: Jen Jenson; Director of Product Development: Spencer Brinker; Managing Editor: Allison Juda; Editor: Cole Nelson; Associate Editor: Naomi Reich; Associate Editor: Tiana Tran; Art Director: Colin O'Dea; Designer: Kim Jones; Designer: Kayla Eggert; Product Development Specialist: Owen Hamlin

Statement on Usage of Generative Artificial Intelligence
Bearport Publishing remains committed to publishing high-quality nonfiction books. Therefore, we restrict the use of generative AI to ensure accuracy of all text and visual components pertaining to a book's subject. See BearportPublishing.com for details.

Library of Congress Cataloging-in-Publication Data is available at www.loc.gov or upon request from the publisher.

ISBN: 979-8-89232-648-3 (hardcover)
ISBN: 979-8-89232-681-0 (ebook)

Copyright © 2025 Bearport Publishing Company. All rights reserved. No part of this publication may be reproduced in whole or in part, stored in any retrieval system, or transmitted in any form or by any means, electronic, mechanical, photocopying, recording, or otherwise, without written permission from the publisher.

For more information, write to Bearport Publishing, 5357 Penn Avenue South, Minneapolis, MN 55419.

CONTENTS

The World of Gaming 4

Acting without a Stage: Voice Actor 6

Like and Subscribe: Streamer 8

Setting the Standards: Game Designer 10

Character Sketching: Concept Artist 12

Creative Leader: Producer 14

Inventing Worlds: Writer 16

Do You Hear That? Sound Designer 18

Bringing Games to Life: Programmer 20

Going Pro: Esports Player 22

Finding Bugs: Game Tester 24

Guide to Victory: Esports Coach 26

Making Make-Believe 28

Gaming Careers Spotlight: Shigeru Miyamoto. 29

Glossary 30

Read More 31

Learn More Online 31

Index 32

About the Author 32

THE WORLD OF GAMING

Many people spend their free time playing video games for fun. But some have turned this pastime into a career. In fact, gaming is a huge **industry** full of many different jobs. From designing new games to playing **professionally**, there's a career for everyone who loves video games. Let's plug into the world of gaming jobs on the edge!

One of the best-selling games of all time is *Tetris*. It has sold more than 500 million copies since its release in 1985.

ACTING WITHOUT A STAGE

Voice Actor

Voice actors bring game characters to life! These unseen heroes study a script to get to know their roles. Then, they **rehearse** their lines to find the best voices for their characters. These actors sometimes do more than just speak. Voice actors may also make the sound effects for when their characters do things such as take a punch or jump over things.

What It Takes

- ☑ A background in theater
- ☑ An openness to feedback
- ☑ A wide vocal range
- ☑ Strong lungs
- ☑ Confidence

Some voice actors provide **dubbing** for game characters originally recorded in a different language.

It takes hours for most voice actors to record their lines.

Many voice actors record from home, using their own microphones and other personal equipment.

LIKE AND SUBSCRIBE

Streamer

Streamers are gamers who **livestream** themselves for viewers all around the world. However, these players do more than just beat the game. They also work hard to build their online communities. Streamers do this by interacting with viewers, playing game requests, and answering audience questions. A growing viewership can eventually lead to **brand deals**. This is when gamers get paid to run advertisements or use specific gear while streaming.

What It Takes

- ☑ An ability to sit for long hours
- ☑ Great communication
- ☑ Attention to detail
- ☑ A good sense of humor

Streamers often edit and publish their content after a livestream.

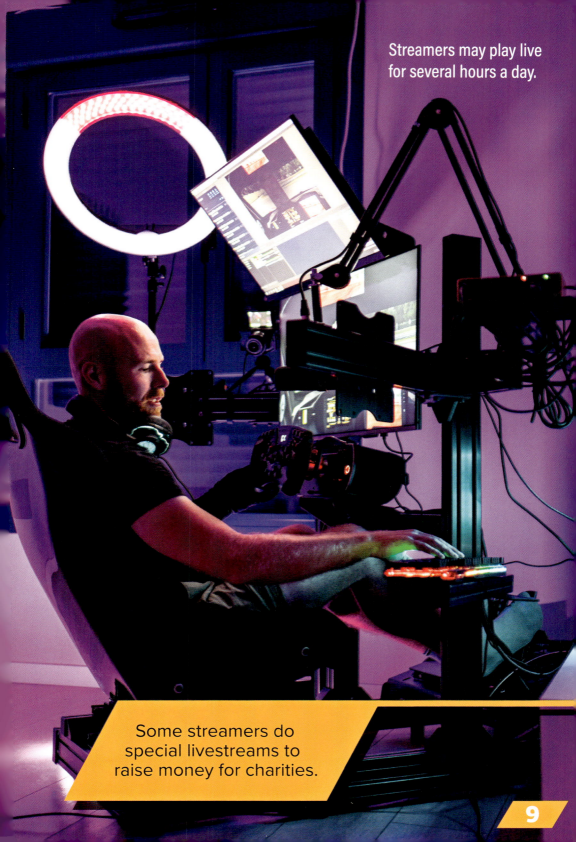

Streamers may play live for several hours a day.

Some streamers do special livestreams to raise money for charities.

9

SETTING THE STANDARDS

Game Designer

Game designers are the ones who make games fun. These creative minds are responsible for deciding the rules of a game and figuring out how it is played. They also think up interactive elements. This includes the obstacles players face or objectives they must meet in the game. Additionally, game designers determine how easy or hard it may be for players to win.

What It Takes

- ☑ An ability to brainstorm
- ☑ Strong teamwork
- ☑ Programming skills
- ☑ A degree in **software** engineering
- ☑ Attention to detail

How players lose or win the game is part of the designer's job.

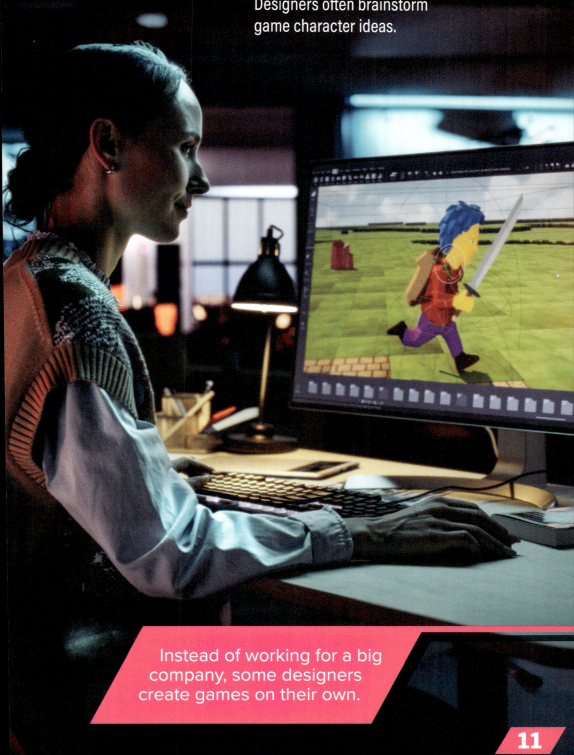

Designers often brainstorm game character ideas.

Instead of working for a big company, some designers create games on their own.

CHARACTER SKETCHING

Concept Artist

A concept artist is someone who imagines and sketches out different game elements. They're responsible for visualizing every part of a game—characters, weapons, and even all the cool places a player might visit. While some concept artists start by sketching on paper, most have gone completely digital. The concepts they create are **referenced** by other departments throughout the **development** process.

What It Takes

- ☑ A steady hand
- ☑ A love of drawing
- ☑ Computer skills
- ☑ A lively imagination
- ☑ World-building skills

These artists create both two-dimensional and three-dimensional art.

Concept artists often use tablets to make digital art.

Sometimes, concept artists must create many detailed sketches on very tight deadlines.

CREATIVE LEADER

Producer

Producers manage the creation of a video game from beginning to end. They are responsible for keeping track of budgets and setting project timelines for the development team to follow. These leaders make sure everything stays on schedule. Producers are also the bridge between different departments, helping with communication and cooperation throughout the game development process.

What It Takes

- ☑ Strong communication skills
- ☑ Leadership
- ☑ Being good with numbers
- ☑ Time management skills

Producers sometimes speak at press events for the game.

Producers often meet with the development team to keep everyone on track.

Sometimes, producers will help create parts of a game's story.

INVENTING WORLDS

Writer

The storylines in today's games are more complex and detailed than ever before. Depending on a player's choices, games may have multiple endings—sometimes even more than 10! This would not be possible without skilled writers. These pros have the job of developing not only the main story of the game, but also other in-game content. This may include detailed character backstories, personalities, and **dialogue**.

What It Takes

- ☑ Strong writing skills
- ☑ Publishing experience
- ☑ Lots of creativity
- ☑ Being open to different opinions
- ☑ Good time management

Writers work with game designers to craft the perfect storyline.

Game writers create the script that voice actors use.

Writers do research to come up with diverse characters and unique story elements.

DO YOU HEAR THAT?

Sound Designer

As their name suggests, sound designers are in charge of every single sound in a game! One part of their job includes searching for the perfect sound effects to match character actions. Another is finding or creating background music that plays throughout a game. But their job doesn't end there. Sound designers also record and edit the dialogue of voice actors.

What It Takes

- ☑ A love of music
- ☑ A knowledge of different sounds
- ☑ Experience with audio engineering software
- ☑ Good listening skills
- ☑ Attention to detail

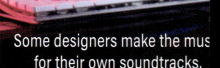

Some designers make the music for their own soundtracks.

Sometimes, sound designers have to make unique sound effects from scratch.

Sound designers add realistic sound effects to improve the gaming experience.

BRINGING GAMES TO LIFE

Programmer

Programmers are experts at using software to create all kinds of video games. They write code to bring the games to life! If the player needs to fight in a game, programmers make it happen. These computer whizzes work closely with other teams to ensure all parts of a game run smoothly. Programmers also tackle any problems that come up during the development process, such as long loading times.

What It Takes

- ✓ Teamwork
- ✓ Problem-solving skills
- ✓ Computer programming experience
- ✓ Time-management skills

A programmer needs to make games work on different platforms.

Programmers often work on content updates and **bug** fixes for completed games.

Unity and Java are two of the most popular game engines programmers use in their work.

GOING PRO

Esports Player

Esports players are the best gamers on the planet. Unlike casual players, they play on a professional level. Esports players often train more than 50 hours a week—by playing games! They must know how a game works and perfect their own gameplay. This allows them to develop new **strategies** for competitions, where they put their skills to the test.

What It Takes

- ✓ An ability to stay calm under pressure
- ✓ Intense concentration
- ✓ A competitive nature
- ✓ Great hand-eye coordination
- ✓ A strategic mind

Professional gamers compete in esports matches in front of live audiences.

Esports teams receive trophies and prize money after winning major tournaments.

Most esports games are team-oriented. They usually have five players on each team.

23

FINDING BUGS

Game Tester

Imagine playing a supercool new game before everyone else. That's what game testers do! It's their job to play games that are still **under development**. They play the same game over and over again. Each time, the testers take different paths or interact with different objects. These gamers then write reports on any bugs they find so developers know what to fix.

What It Takes

- ☑ An ability to sit for long hours
- ☑ Attention to detail
- ☑ Quick fingers for smashing buttons
- ☑ Being organized
- ☑ A passion for games

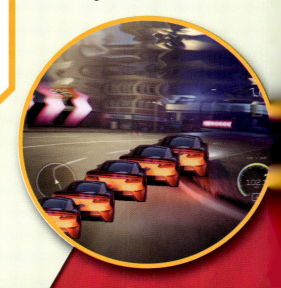

Game testers look for **glitches** in a game's software.

A game tester must explore every feature of a game.

Some game testers focus on the user experience by testing how easy or hard a game is to play.

25

GUIDE TO VICTORY

Esports Coach

Did you know that like with other sports, most esports teams also have coaches? Esports coaches do everything they can to help their team win. These leaders recruit new talent, analyze game footage, provide players with feedback, and come up with new strategies for the team. This coach keeps the gaming team on track!

What It Takes

- ☑ Strong leadership skills
- ☑ Attention to detail
- ☑ An eye for talent
- ☑ A passion for gaming

Watching past games helps coaches develop future plans.

Esports coaches know the strengths and weaknesses of each player.

Not all esports coaches are gamers themselves. But they still need to know everything about the game.

MAKING MAKE-BELIEVE

There are so many other different gaming jobs out there! Whether it's designing supercool art or writing unique storylines, gaming career workers love doing what they do. Their creative minds and strong determination bring games to life for millions of players—making the industry what it is today.

28

GAMING CAREERS SPOTLIGHT

Shigeru Miyamoto

Shigeru Miyamoto is a video game designer who is famous for his amazing work on popular games like *Super Mario Brothers* and *The Legend of Zelda*. He has designed games for every Nintendo system, including **arcade** machines and home **consoles**. His games have made Nintendo a huge success and inspired other designers to follow in his footsteps.

GLOSSARY

arcade a place where people can go to play video games

brand deals partnerships between content creators and brands

bug an unexpected flaw in software

consoles devices that are used to play video games

development the act of creating something

dialogue conversation between two or more people in a game, book, play, or movie

dubbing replacing dialogue in a different language

glitches minor malfunctions in software

industry the businesses or companies that make, sell, or trade things to make money

livestream an event that is played over the internet in real time

professionally in a way that relates to people who do something for a job

referenced used as a source of information in order to learn something

rehearse practice a play, piece of music, or other work for a performance

software a computer program that performs a set of tasks

strategies the ways a team plays and scores points or stops other teams from scoring

under development in the process of being prepared or completed

READ MORE

Light, Charley. *Online Gaming (The Internet Safety Handbook).* Buffalo, NY: Enslow Publishing, 2024.

Polinsky, Paige V. *Nintendo (Blastoff! Discovery. Behind the Brand).* Minneapolis: Bellwether Media, 2023.

Schwartz, Heather E. *Esports Careers (Lerner Sports. Esports Zone).* Minneapolis: Lerner Publications, 2024.

LEARN MORE ONLINE

1. Go to **FactSurfer.com** or scan the QR code below.
2. Enter "**Gaming Careers**" into the search box.
3. Click on the cover of this book to see a list of websites.

INDEX

audiences 8, 22
bugs 21, 24
coaches 26–27
concept artists 12–13
consoles 29
esports 22–23, 26–27
game designers 10–11, 16, 29
gamers 8, 22, 24, 27
glitches 24
industry 4, 28
Miyamato, Shigeru 29
Nintendo 29
players 8, 10, 12, 16, 20, 22–23, 26–27
producers 14–15
programmers 20–21
sound designers 18–19
streamers 8–9
testers 24–25
voice actors 6–7, 17–18
writers 16–17

ABOUT THE AUTHOR

J. G. Minyard is an author who lives with his two cats in Minneapolis. He enjoys reading, writing, basketball, and video games.